To the Reader...

Our purpose in creating this series is to provide young readers with accurate accounts of the lives of Native American men and women important in the history of their tribes. The stories are written by scholars, including American Indians.

Native Americans are as much a part of North American life today as they were one hundred years ago. Even in times past, Indians were not all the same. Not all of them lived in teepees or wore feather · warbonnets. They were not all warriors. Some did fight against the white man, but many befriended him.

Whether patriot or politician, athlete or artist, Arapaho or Zuni, the story of each person in this series deserves to be told. Whether the individuals gained distinction on the battlefield or the playing field, in the courtroom or the classroom, they have enriched the heritage and history of all Americans. It is hoped that those who read their stories will realize that many different peoples, regardless of culture or color, have played a part in shaping the United States and Canada, in making both countries what they are today.

Herman J. Viola
General Editor
Author of *Exploring the West*
and other volumes on the West
and Native Americans

GENERAL EDITOR
Herman J. Viola
Author of *Exploring the West* and other volumes on the West
and American Indians

MANAGING EDITOR
Robert M. Kvasnicka
Coeditor of *The Commissioners of Indian Affairs, 1824–1977*
Coeditor of *Indian-White Relations: A Persistent Paradox*

MANUSCRIPT EDITOR
Barbara J. Behm

DESIGNER
Kathleen A. Hartnett

PRODUCTION
Andrew Rupniewski
Eileen Rickey

First Steck-Vaughn Edition 1993
Copyright © 1990 Pinnacle Press, Inc. doing business as Rivilo
Books

Library of Congress Number: 89-10410

  4 5 6 7 8 9   95 94 93 92

Library of Congress Cataloging-in-Publication Data

Lowe, Felix C.
   John Ross.
   (Raintree American Indian stories)
   Summary: Discusses the Cherokee chief who fought
unsuccessfully to protect the land of his people, until they were
forced to march along the Trail of Tears to Oklahoma.
   1. Ross, John, 1790-1866—Juvenile literature.   2. Cherokee
Indians—Biography—Juvenile literature.   3. Indians of North
America—Georgia—Biography.   4. Indians of North America—
Oklahoma—Biography.   [1. Ross, John, 1790-1866.   2. Cherokee
Indians—Biography.   3. Indians of North America—Biography]
I. Title.   II. Series.
E99.C5R6745   1989   973′.0497502   [B]   [92]   89-10410
ISBN 0-8172-3407-1   hardcover library binding
ISBN 0-8114-4093-1   softcover binding

JOHN ROSS

Text by Felix C. Lowe
Illustrations by Patrick Soper

A RIVILO BOOK

RSVP
RAINTREE
STECK-VAUGHN
PUBLISHERS
The Steck-Vaughn Company

John Ross was principal chief of the Cherokee Nation for nearly forty years. Under his leadership, the tribe survived a terrible forced removal from its homeland and the devastating effects of the Civil War. Although he was only one-eighth Cherokee by blood, John Ross felt one hundred percent American Indian. He was proud to have served both his people and the government of the United States.

The Cherokee tribe belonged to a group known as the Civilized Tribes. The others were the Creeks, the Choctaw, and the Chickasaw. These tribes hoped that by learning to live like the whites they would be able to keep their lands. As a result, many members of these tribes married whites. They took on white customs and gave up their Indian lifestyle. Many of them became farmers, cattlemen, and merchants.

John Ross was a member of one of the mixed-blood Cherokee families. He was born on October 3, 1790, in Turkey Town, Alabama. His parents, Daniel and Mollie, had settled there two years earlier. Mollie was part Cherokee, but Daniel came from Scotland. Soon after John's birth, his parents moved to Georgia. His earliest memories were of living in a log cabin in the middle of the Cherokee Indians.

John's parents believed that their children should have a good education. John's first lessons were by the fireplace in his home. At the age of nine, he and his brothers studied with a tutor. Later John attended Kingston Academy in Tennessee.

As a child, his Cherokee name was *Tsan Usdi*, which means "Little John." When he was grown, he was given a new name according to Cherokee custom. He was called *Kooweskoowe*, the name of a rare migratory bird. This fit him because he made many trips while doing tribal business for the Cherokee.

As a young man, John became part owner of a store that supplied goods to the Cherokee. In 1812, the government hired John to deliver supplies to the nearly two thousand Cherokee who had moved west of the Mississippi River into Arkansas. The trip was difficult and exciting. John narrowly escaped a gang of murderers, his boat was wrecked, and he ended up having to walk about two hundred miles before reaching the end of his journey.

During the War of 1812, John served as a second lieutenant with a company of mounted Cherokee. His company helped General Andrew Jackson defeat the Creek Indians at Horseshoe Bend in 1813. Almost eight hundred Creek Indians were killed in the battle that killed only twenty-six white soldiers. From that, John realized that no Indian tribe would ever be as strong as the United States Army.

John also decided that he did not want to be a soldier, and he quickly left the military after the Creek campaign. Shortly afterward, he married Elizabeth Brown Henley who was called Quatie. Little is known about her, but she probably was a full-blood Cherokee. She and John had six children.

The Cherokee Nation included sections of Alabama, Georgia, North Carolina, and Tennessee. More than eight thousand Cherokee lived in Georgia. The white Georgians who wanted the Indians to leave the state expected the United States government to force the Cherokee to join those already living in the West. The government made treaties with the Cherokee providing for their removal, but few Indians moved west. Instead, the Cherokee took steps to strengthen their position in their homeland, where they had built roads, constructed schools and churches, and set up businesses.

Having decided that they would sell no more land to the whites, the Cherokee established a central government similar to that of the United States. The tribe's sense of national identity was made stronger by the use of an alphabet or syllabary (a listing of syllables). This allowed the Cherokee to read and write in their own language. Publication of the *Cherokee Phoenix,* a national newspaper written in English and Cherokee, began in 1828. Elias Boudinot, the editor, used the paper to publish the Nation's laws and public documents, as well as news stories.

John Ross was a part of the new government from the beginning. He held one of the important legislative positions. He made several trips to Washington, D.C., on tribal business. In 1827, he moved to a farm about thirty miles from New Echota, the new capital of the Cherokee Nation. There he built a beautiful home with tall brick chimneys and twenty glass windows. By the mid-1830s, he was a typical Southern planter. He also operated a profitable ferry business on the Coosa River.

In 1828, the Cherokee Nation's legislature selected Ross to be the Nation's principal chief. This position was similar to that of the president of the United States. Ross was an unlikely leader of the Cherokee Indians. He was short and stocky. He did not look like an Indian. He did not speak the Cherokee language very well. But because he was raised among them, he understood the Cherokee and their way of life. He knew how important their homelands were to them. Most Cherokee trusted him completely. John Ross was well prepared to be their champion.

The same year that Ross was chosen chief, Andrew Jackson became president of the United States. Jackson was from Tennessee, which was still occupied in part by the Cherokee and Chickasaw Indians. He was determined to stop Indian ownership of lands east of the Mississippi River. He wanted the Indians to move west. If they did not, they would come under the laws of the United States. As president, Jackson recommended that Congress pass laws to remove the Indians. Many whites protested, but the Indian Removal Act became law in 1830.

The Georgia legislature took Jackson's election as a signal to pass laws allowing Georgia to take some of the Cherokee lands and to hold state laws over the tribe. After gold was discovered in the area in July 1829, the Georgians were even more determined that the Cherokee move. In 1830, Georgia passed additional laws suspending the tribe's legislature and courts. A military unit called the Georgia Guard was created for use against the Indians.

Ross and the Cherokee asked for help from both the president and Congress, but they received none. Ross then decided to use the courts to challenge Georgia's actions. Two famous cases, *Cherokee Nation* v. *Georgia* and *Worcester* v. *Georgia,* were taken to the Supreme Court. The Court was sympathetic to the Cherokee. Its ruling on the second case said that all of Georgia's actions against the Cherokee were against the law. The United States was actually responsible for protecting the tribe.

Ross and the Cherokee were overjoyed by the court's decision, but their happiness did not last long. President Jackson made it clear that he would not enforce the Supreme Court's ruling. The Georgia officials were able to continue their cruel treatment of the Cherokee.

Some influential Cherokee Indians began to think that the tribe should sell its lands and move west. The leaders of these Indians were Major Ridge, his son, John, and his nephew, Elias Boudinot. They were afraid that Georgia and the other states would take their lands for nothing.

In 1833, whites began taking over the Cherokee lands. They forced the Indians out of their homes. Ross was able to hold them off for a time. One spring evening in 1835, however, he returned from a trip to Washington, D.C., to find a white family living in his home. His farm and ferry business were lost to the whites. Ross took his sick wife and the children and moved to Red Clay, Tennessee, just across the Georgia border. There they lived in a simple one-room cabin.

Even after Ross moved to Tennessee, he continued to be troubled by Georgia officials. In November 1835, members of the Georgia Guard crossed into Tennessee and arrested him. He was taken back to Georgia where he was held in jail for thirteen days. No charges were brought against him, and he was finally released.

By this time, Ross realized that the Cherokee probably would have to move. When he got out of jail, he went to Washington, D.C. There he discussed the best terms for the removal. Back in the Cherokee Nation, a federal government agent took advantage of Ross's absence. The agent made a treaty with Ridge's pro-removal group. According to the treaty, the Cherokee agreed to sell their lands for five million dollars. They were to leave for the west within three years. When they signed the treaty, the Ridge group broke a Cherokee law. By selling tribal lands without the entire Nation's consent, they committed a crime. This crime was punishable by death.

Ross felt betrayed. What he feared most had happened. A small group of Cherokee Indians had pledged the entire Nation to removal. Despite protests from hundreds of white citizens, the United States Senate approved the treaty. It became law in 1836. All of Ross's efforts to stop the treaty or to make a better one for the Cherokee were unsuccessful. In March 1838, he presented a petition to Congress that was signed by approximately fifteen thousand Cherokee who were against removal. The document was ignored.

Only about two thousand Cherokee moved west on their own. General Scott and seven thousand troops arrived in the Cherokee Nation to forcibly remove the rest. The soldiers rounded up the Cherokee and held them in stockades until the journey could begin.

The final departure point was Ross's Landing, present-day Chattanooga, Tennessee. Ross received federal permission to help plan the move. The tribe was divided into thirteen groups of about one thousand people each. The trip took about six months. More than four thousand Cherokee died during the terrible journey.

One of those who died was Quatie, John's wife. The weak but unselfish woman had given her only blanket to a sick child who needed protection from the sleet and snow of an early winter storm. The Cherokee referred to the journey as "The Trail Where They Cried." It is more commonly called "The Trail of Tears."

Life for John Ross and the Cherokee in their new country (present-day Oklahoma) was not easy at first. The government was supposed to give the Cherokee food and supplies for one year, but what they received was not enough. Often the beef was unfit to eat. The corn was weighed incorrectly by dishonest white men. Finally, the Cherokee were given approval to buy their own supplies. The beef ration of one dollar per month per person, however, bought very little at the high prices they were charged.

Ross also faced many other problems. He had to continue to deal with the federal government to make sure that the Cherokee received the money due them. At the same time, his leadership within the Cherokee Nation was being challenged by two different groups of Cherokee. One group was the western Cherokee, called the Old Settlers, who had moved to Oklahoma from Arkansas. The other group was Ridge's Treaty Party. Neither of these groups wanted Ross as their leader. They united in opposing him.

In 1839, these groups became even more firm about setting up their own government when some men from Ross's group murdered Major Ridge, John Ridge, and Elias Boudinot. The three men were killed because they had sold the tribal lands without the tribe's consent. Ross was not responsible for the deaths, but his enemies thought he was. This conflict within the tribe hurt Ross's efforts in Washington, D.C., because some officials did not recognize him as chief of the entire Cherokee Nation.

In 1844, John married for a second time. His bride was Mary Bryan Stapler, a Quaker from Delaware. She was thirty-six years younger than Ross. Ross took his wife to his new home called Rose Cottage. It was a beautiful two-story house set at the end of a long drive bordered with rose bushes. He and Mary had two children.

In 1846, Ross's attempts to keep unity in the Nation and to get money for property the Cherokee lost met with success. Ross persuaded President James K. Polk to form a committee to investigate the claims of the three different groups of Cherokee. The committee came to an agreement that satisfied the Old Settlers, Ridge's Treaty Party, and Ross's group. The Treaty of 1846 preserved the unity of the Cherokee Nation, Ross's primary goal. It started a period of calm that lasted for more than a dozen years.

In spite of the political problems, the Cherokee made progress in their new country. The capital was established at Tahlequah. A new tribal newspaper, the *Cherokee Advocate,* was started. An educational system was set up with eleven public schools. Ross was particularly proud of the male and female high schools, called seminaries, that opened in 1851. His plans also included the construction of a national library, but there was never enough money to build it.

Cherokee unity was shattered by the Civil War. Once again the tribe split. This time, it was over the issues of slavery and loyalty to the United States. Because the Cherokee Nation had treaty and financial ties with the United States, Ross favored the Union. But many Cherokee were slaveholders, and most of them supported the Southern cause. Ross hoped the Cherokee Nation could remain neutral during the war. When the surrounding Indian tribes allied themselves with the Confederacy, Ross reluctantly advised the Cherokee to side with the Confederate States. With Confederate troops so close to the Cherokee Nation, his decision was a practical one.

When Union forces invaded the Cherokee Nation, Ross and his family went north. He went to Washington, D.C., where he hoped to find help for his people. He asked that Union troops be stationed within the Cherokee Nation to protect the loyal Cherokee from the Confederate forces. He also had to convince federal officials that he was not a traitor. Circumstances had forced him to ally the Cherokee Nation with the Confederacy.

Meanwhile, the Cherokee Nation had become a vast battleground. About nine thousand Cherokee loyal to the Union were uprooted from their homes, losing everything. Schools, public buildings, and churches were burned and destroyed in the fighting. Ross's home, Rose Cottage, was burned to the ground by Confederate Cherokee troops led by Stan Watie, the brother of Elias Boudinot. Ross received another blow after the war ended when his wife died of lung congestion.

Ross spent his final days in Washington, D.C., fighting a group led by Stan Watie for control of the Cherokee Nation. It was Ross who won the final victory. The tribe remained united. The treaty of July 19, 1866, identifies Ross as the "Principal Chief of the Cherokee."

Ross died in Washington, D.C., on August 1, 1866. For nearly forty years, he had fought for and preserved the Cherokee Nation. He was buried in the Ross cemetery near the ruins of Rose Cottage.

His story and the history of the Cherokee people are woven together forever.

HISTORY OF JOHN ROSS

1790	John Ross was born. Benjamin Franklin died.
1812	John Ross undertook a long and dangerous trip to deliver supplies to the Cherokee in the West.
1812-1814	Great Britain and the United States fought the War of 1812.
1828	The Cherokee Nation's legislature elected John Ross to be principal chief.
1829	Gold is discovered in Georgia.
1830	The Indian Removal Act is passed by Congress allowing the government to move the Eastern tribes west of the Mississippi River.
1835	John Ross lost his home, farm, and business to whites.
1836	The treaty made with the United States government by a small group of Cherokee Indians became law, committing the Cherokee Nation to move west of the Mississippi River.
1838-1839	The Cherokee were forcibly removed to Indian Territory, a journey popularly known as the "Trail of Tears."
1860	The pony express begins.
1861-1865	The Civil War is fought between the North and the South.
1866	A treaty reestablishing relations between the United States government and the Cherokee following the Civil War recognized John Ross as "Principal Chief of the Cherokee."
	John Ross died on August 1. Alfred Nobel invented dynamite, laying the foundation for the fortune that allowed him to establish the Nobel prizes.